The
Guilt Intervention

Disclaimer

This book is for people struggling with guilt. There are occasions in which both guilt and shame are triggered, and it is important to understand the difference before reading this book. *The Guilt Intervention*, or The Process will allow you to eradicate guilt and build a new framework in which you perceive guilt and stop it from generalizing into your life.

There is a separate process for shame, but it may not always be easily accessible without additional professional support due to the complexity and layers of shame.

To increase your success with this book, it is important to only use it with guilt.

Prologue

What is the difference between guilt and shame? I am glad you asked. Guilt is when someone feels bad about an action or behavior they committed, whereas shame is the negative core belief there is something wrong with the self, such as, "I am bad," "I am useless," "I am fat," "I am broken," etc. Sometimes, guilt and shame might be activated together, however depending on the triggering event, if the event is not processed, the guilt or shame could generalize into other parts of your life. If you want to process a triggering event with shame and guilt, try to separate the behaviors from the belief systems. Once separated, focus only on the feelings of guilt and note the shame as that is still helpful information to explore with a mental health professional.

For example, Teresa is a middle school teacher, and in her first year of teaching, one of her students was being disrespectful to her and other peers. Teresa pulled the student outside and addressed the student with a hostile tone. She was later reprimanded by her superior, and she felt intense feelings of guilt and shame. To use The Process, Teresa separated the triggering event by exploring where she felt guilty and ashamed.

Teresa felt guilty for her tone and choice of words towards the student and felt shame for being reprimanded herself. Teresa's feelings of shame were activated by the reprimand because she believed that she was a bad person. This reinforced a core belief that people won't love her if she is not perfect.

Teresa was able to process the guilt on her own but required me to help separate and process the shame separately.

If you find yourself with a similar example in which you feel both guilt and shame, note the behaviors that make you feel guilty and apply The Process. Then seek professional help to process the feelings and beliefs associated with shame.

May this book be a beacon of hope and empower you to regain your happiness.

Contents

Contents

Introduction

C an you imagine a world without unhealthy guilt? If you had a process to let go of guilt, would you do it? If you are reading this book, it's because something has happened where you made a decision, a series of actions– or lack of actions– that you cannot take back. If you are struggling with guilt, this is a process that will allow you to transform those feelings into actions that will empower you. There are many challenges we face regarding change, but without the right process, tools, or guidance, it can be difficult to make any notable progress.

It is widely accepted by mental health professionals that there are two types of guilt: persecutory guilt and reparative guilt. Persecutory guilt can be toxic and can develop emotional stagnation because there is no emotional flow or shift in perspective. Reparative guilt, however, can have healing components that allow growth and movement forward from the triggering event.

Guilt emotions are a natural way our bodies process and communicate information to the self. There are no bad emotions-- guilt is a natural emotion with its own specific purpose. It's easy to get caught up in pursuing happiness, so we might neglect or avoid feeling anything else. Ask yourself: how do you perceive depression, anxiety, fear, shame or guilt? What has influenced your belief systems around these emotions? Do you have any stigmas around these emotions? If so, what are they? How did you come to those conclusions? Do you allow emotions to flow and transition, or do you hold on to them?

From the moment we are born, we are constantly transitioning to new phases of our life– growth, experiential, school, jobs, relationships, etc.

Life is a constant state of transitions.

If we fail to transition throughout our lives mentally, emotionally, or from an experience, it may develop a sense of stagnation that could create additional negative symptoms.

Emotions are meant to flow and transition as they are activated. Unlike thoughts, feelings don't have rationality; they just exist. It is up to the conscious mind to incorporate a mental filter or a belief system that then integrates that emotion as a positive or negative experience. However, through our upbringing, life experiences, and societal influences, we have our own associations that lead us to perceive thoughts or emotions in a certain way. The conscious effort is when you actively take the information provided by your body and mind, then are mindful and purposeful to choose what you do with the information. The Process will be your intervention to move your perceptions, associations, and emotional responses to the conscious mind, where you can then choose how to integrate the information.

Before we jump into The Process, let's explore how we integrate and associate information that influences emotional flow and emotional stagnation.

First, we have the triggering event or interaction. Our minds capture the information of what is happening with no judgment; the information at this point is neutral. Once our mind makes sense of the event, we create a perceived outcome and/or assumption of what we think is happening based on previous experiences. Next, this information gets passed down to our nervous system, stimulating an emotional and physical response (this could be positive or negative).

Finally, we have a new association of how we will continue to perceive and react to future similar events.

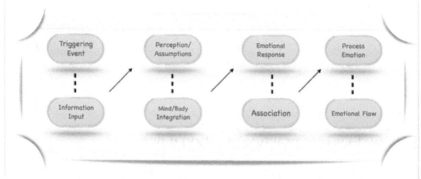

If an emotion is repressed, avoided, or compartmentalized over a long period, we can develop emotional stagnation, where the emotion is trapped without healing. Over time these emotions can manifest into headaches, muscle tension, back pain, restless sleep, etc. that may not have a medical explanation. Emotional stagnation can also trigger underlying depression, anger, irritability, anxiety, or numbness. We experience emotional stagnation due to our defense mechanisms. A defense mechanism is a mental filter created, usually from a young age, and protects our ego from any negative experience. This is a barrier to processing the information, leading to emotional stagnation. Some examples include avoidance, denial, justification, rationalization, deflection, minimization, etc. The Process bypasses the defense mechanisms, helps to increase emotional flow, and aids in the prevention of emotional stagnation.

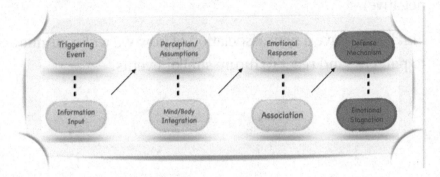

So how does one practice emotional flow?

First, explore and challenge your beliefs around any personal stigmas, and create a healthier way to perceive negative emotions. Observe your inner world and listen without judgment.

Second, practice sitting with your emotions. Be comfortable feeling sad or anxious-- remember that no emotion lasts forever. This might be difficult, so start with something less triggering, or practice with someone you feel comfortable with, including a health professional if needed.

Finally, incorporate a mindset of growth and resiliency that allows you to move towards healing. This could be a new outlook towards processing or letting go of emotions. Explore and address defense mechanisms and reframe negative automatic thoughts and behaviors to help reshape how you perceive your reality.

There are two ways to work through The Process: by reading through the entire book and learning about The Process first or read and work through each step as you go; do whatever feels more comfortable and beneficial to you.

Whether you are a caregiver, a parent, have lost a loved one, struggle to say no sometimes, and are feeling guilty, The Process is for you.

Chapter 1
The Process

Once upon a time, there was a fisherman named Frank. Frank would walk to a small pond every day and catch a few fish each day. It was the perfect amount for him and his family. After a while, he realized he would like to catch bigger fish to avoid having to fish every day, to spend more time with his family. One day he took a different route to change up his daily routine. He came across a small food market and saw another fisherman carrying one of the biggest fish he'd ever laid eyes upon.

"Wow, where did you catch this giant fish?" Frank asked. The other fisherman responded, "If you keep walking up the hill, you'll see a river that flows as far as the eye can see."

Frank was ecstatic. He walked as fast as he could to see this river for himself without hesitation.

"What a beautiful sight," he thought to himself. Wasting no time, he cast his rod and waited.

An hour passed and nothing.

He felt desperate and frustrated. Before he realized it, it was dawn and he had no fish to show. Feeling defeated and hopeless, he walked back home to his starving family. Frank felt guilt, regret, and selfishness for trying to do something for himself that eventually caused his family to be hungry that day.

The next day, still feeling guilty and upset, Frank went back to the market to confront the other fisherman and yelled, "Hey! You lied to me. You said I could catch fish in that river and all you did was waste my time!" The other fisherman replied, "Sorry you feel that way, but fishing at a pond and at a river are very different. Have you tried changing your lures? Did you try different bait? Have you tried different hooks or techniques?"

Frank paused and realized he hadn't tried anything different; he had assumed that his same process would work in any body of water. Frank the fisherman wanted the change, he was motivated and made an effort, but his efforts were futile given that he was missing one of the most important things: the process.

I commend you for doing this on your own, but you could be setting yourself up for failure without all the components. Worse, similar to Frank the fisherman, it could reinforce not wanting to try again, create a sense of defeat, hopelessness or other negative belief systems. Guilt has been a part of our lives for a long time and is influenced by societal, cultural, and religious values. I hope this book can offer you hope, insight, and tools to guide you through these difficult times. I strongly believe everyone can heal themselves from within if they have the appropriate tools.

The 9-step Process uses an analytical, behavioral, and logical approach that will challenge your perceived outcome, feelings, and thoughts and then allow you to shift towards reparative guilt and possibly not feel guilty at all for that triggering event.

The Process also incorporates the activation of the left and right brain hemispheres. Each hemisphere has its own set of principles and works simultaneously. For example, left-brain-dominant individuals are more logical and analytical, and the right-brain-dominant individuals are more creative and spontaneous. There are exceptions, which is a simplification, but "left brain" individuals might learn or process information differently from "right brain" individuals.

Great news! Regardless of your processing approach or personality characteristics, The Process activates both parts of the brain and allow you to simultaneously process the triggering event from a logical and emotional aspect. Each step has been designed to quickly shift from the left to right part of the brain to maintain brain activity and engagement and facilitate a shift in the perceived outcome.

Let's take a quick look at the 9 steps of The Process.

Step One: Triggering Event

Step Two: Automatic Statements of the Perceived Outcome

Step Three: Feelings & Physical Sensations (Baseline)

Step Four: Activating Statement

Step Five: Accountability Statement

Step Six: Self-Compassion & Affirmation Statements

Step Seven: Awareness

Step Eight: Self-Growth Agreements

Step Nine: Feelings & Physical Sensations (Shifted)

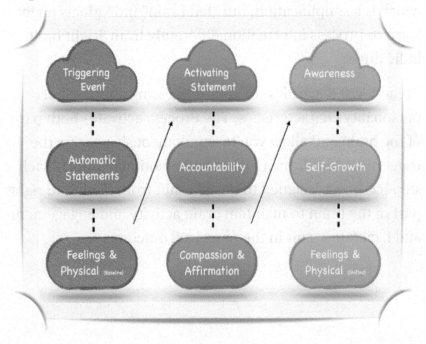

The **triggering event** is the situation or interaction followed by an action or a lack thereof that later created feelings of guilt, leaving you with a perceived outcome of the event. The perceived outcome is how you feel or view triggering events from the past. The Process will help you shift your perspective to a healthier and more rational outcome.

Statements of the perceived outcome are automatic thoughts associated with feelings of guilt. Life comprises simple thoughts that can influence a decision or an emotional response. However, not all thoughts are rational or factual, and if we don't make the conscious effort to check them, they can influence how we live our life.

The triggering event will cause **feelings and physical sensations** associated with automatic thoughts and the perceived outcome. These are the baseline emotions compared to the new shifted emotions after completing The Process. To practice getting this information, learn how to body scan (detailed later).

The **activating statement** is the main guilt statement you will structure into one sentence to prevent cycling, fleeting, or rapid thoughts that can flood your emotions and hinder your ability to shift towards healing.

The **accountability statement** separates the factual behaviors that each party is responsible for and helps gain clarity of the actions done. These must be specific statements.

Self-compassion & affirmation statements are the emotional approach to practicing kindness and showing grace to the self. They are self-affirming statements that demonstrate compassion and self-empathy. These statements should neutralize the feelings of guilt. They should not justify or minimize the accountability statement. A good rule of thumb is to think of what you would tell a friend or family member if they were in your situation.

Awareness statements include the external factors that influenced the actions but are not within our control. This step removes the "I" and "you" statements to help you understand and emphasize the external influences.

Self-growth agreements are the agreements you will make with yourself that will allow emotional flow, a new perceived outcome, and an empowering shift towards healing and reparative guilt. These statements should be specific, realistic, and directly associated with the activating statement.

Finally, to see your results, we will practice body scanning to notice the shifted emotions and physical sensations. Then we will go back and read the activating statement and notice the shift in emotional responses and perceived outcome. Usually, after The Process is completed, the activating statement may not feel rational, proportionate to how it was originally perceived, or have any meaning whatsoever.

You should feel the shift at that point, but it is important to reframe the activating statement into something that feels more accurate to your newly shifted perceived outcome if it applies. We can't change the choices we've made, but we can change how we perceive them.

Are you ready to take action?
Let's own your happiness!

Image

I bump into a dresser and a picture frame falls; an image is shattered.

Now I live with the consequence of broken glass.

Is this something I should pick up or fix up or let it pass?

Regardless, it's all the same, this picture frame will never be the same.

It was my favorite picture, I see it every day, it was an image that carried my name,

it was the image I created for myself and somehow, I sabotage it by bumping and shattering this frame.

Such a clumsy move so careless this is how quickly one can change things.

It saddens me, I can't take it back, this is something I have to live with and accept the fact.

But even if this image is shattered, there's still many more pictures in this room, there's still more to me than one picture in this room, there's still more frames that I can buy and rebuild this picture of myself, I don't always have to cry.

I have to let this go and time will do the rest, I'll just have to build a new image and find a new frame, it'll be for the best.

Somehow this should suffice, but I'll do my best to pick up my pieces... and RISE.

Guilt is the emotional compass of morality.

Chapter 2
Guilt

L et's go back to imagining the world without unhealthy guilt. Healthy guilt is also a natural and necessary emotion to help us recognize our actions that may have caused hurt. Unhealthy guilt is a powerful negative emotion that, if not properly addressed, can lead to symptoms of depression, panic, fear, anxiety, and even thoughts of suicide.

Without a process for unhealthy guilt, it will live rent-free in your mind, and if left long enough, it could generalize to other main parts of your life, including relationships and belief systems. The main purpose of feeling guilt is to instill feelings of remorse. It is your body's way of letting you know that something negative happened outside of societal norms. Feeling guilt is like looking into a broken mirror, where the reflection we see is shifted and disproportionate to how we look. It demonstrates that our perceived actions might be disproportionate to what happened.

*Guilt is the first sign of
an opportunity to grow.*

Over time, many professionals have subcategorized guilt into three forms.

Natural Guilt

- Most common type
- Triggered by casual situations
- Least intrusive
- Fades relatively quick

Telling your partner or friends that you will do something and then fail to complete said task and now you feel some level of guilt.

Toxic Guilt

- Most Harmful type
- Can create self-labels
- Spiral of negative thoughts
- Creates anxiety or depression

If it becomes internalized, it then creates self-labels such as I am a failure, I am useless, I am not worthy, etc.

Existential or Survivor's Guilt

- Associated with death
- Associated with Traumatic experiences
- Triggers nightmares, flashbacks, and fear
- Creates anxiety or depression

It stems from surviving certain circumstances where others don't, especially if someone died that was in a similar situation as you might have been.

However, I have identified an additional fourth type of guilt. It is imposed and not internally created. This type is Reactive Guilt or Gaslight Guilt; this stems from manipulative individuals.

Reactive or Gaslight Guilt

- Includes derogatory and accusatory statements from another individual
- It is Imposed and not internally created
- Victim feels forced to make a different choice to alleviate imposed feelings of guilt
- Creates anxiety or depression

When a victimized individual is receiving statements such as, "I am going to hurt myself," "My life is meaningless without you, "I don't have anyone else," "You are wrong" or "It is all your fault." These statements create an emotional and psychological manipulation that results in unsolicited feelings of guilt.

Let's explore the process in which guilt comes about.

First, there is a triggering event we later perceive to have created feelings of guilt. One way to recognize the thoughts that influence guilt is through thoughts that include or imply "should" or "could." This is where ruminating begins to happen, and thoughts such as, "I wish I would have done something differently," or "I didn't do enough," or "I regret making that choice," or "What have I done?" begin.

Step One: Defining the Triggering Event

We must define what the triggering event is to focus on one particular event at a time. This is the event or situation creating negative feelings of guilt. Guilt might be masked by stronger feelings such as anxiety, depression, or anger. If you don't have a current event actively triggering you, think of a past situation that triggers feelings of guilt right now. While doing this, if you have more than one, choose the one with the highest intensity.

We will explore six case studies that cover the various types of guilt. The information has been modified to protect those identities.

Example One: Dianne

Dianne is a first-time parent with a 3-year-old boy. She has recently experienced guilt due to some of her reactions towards her son. Dianne finds herself increasingly frustrated and has been tenser lately, leading to being more "snappy." Dianne believes she is not a good parent.

Can you guess the type of guilt Dianne is feeling?

_____

Example Two: Martha

Martha was married for 5 years and has a child with her ex-husband. She has since identified herself as in a very negative and abusive relationship and has experienced gaslighting over the years. Martha made the conscious choice to end the marriage as she felt it was unhealthy and unsafe for her to be in the relationship. Upon the divorce, the ex-husband, Michael, made manipulative guilt statements that made Martha feel insecure, guilty, and self-doubt regarding her decision to separate from the marriage.

Can you guess the type of guilt Martha is feeling?

_____

Example Three: Jerry

Jerry has been in a committed relationship but has not been emotionally invested in the relationship. He found himself disengaged at times and his relationship with Joel had been unstable for the last few months. Jerry had an affair and his partner Joel caught him being unfaithful. Joel was very hurt and confronted Jerry about the affair, and it created feelings of guilt that lasted for a long period.

Can you guess the type of guilt Jerry is feeling?

_____

Example Four: Leo

Leo is a retired military veteran who served his country for 8 years. During his deployment, he witnessed his friend die during combat, and despite Leo's attempts to revive his friend, it was futile. Over the years, Leo asks himself questions that instill guilt and has developed severe nightmares, depression, and even suicidal thoughts.

Can you guess the type of guilt Leo is feeling?

_____

Example Five: Rebecca

Rebecca is a passive, introverted individual who likes her own space and needs alone time to re-energize and recover. Rebecca struggles to say no to people mainly because she doesn't want others to feel bad or perceive her as an insensitive person who doesn't care about other people's feelings.

Can you guess the type of guilt Rebecca is feeling?

_____

Example Six: Karen

Karen has been in an on-and-off relationship with her partner Kevin, and they have a child together. Karen is contemplating ending the relationship. However, Kevin has made comments that make her feel guilty about wanting to end the relationship. Karen is exploring whether or not she wants to continue and realizes how Kevin's comments and statements influence her decision.

Can you guess the type of guilt Karen is feeling?

_____

Step Two: Automatic Statements of the Perceived Outcome

Automatic
Statements

This section is part of the activation process of emotions. Note this section is intended to bring up those negative feelings. For some, this might be difficult to process, but it is a healthy practice to feel the emotions for them to flow. After you access the automatic guilt or negative thoughts, notice your body by being aware of physical sensations and emotions. This will be your baseline associated with the activating statement (in step four).

Dianne

Automatic Statements of the Perceived Outcome

"I am a bad parent."

"I shouldn't have yelled."

"I hate that I can't control myself."

"I don't know what I am doing."

The increasing frustrations stem from a lack of control when the child is not behaving or doing something that Dianne wants him to do, which can increase frustrations. A lack of control can also activate feelings of anger that could escalate the level of response. When someone is frustrated, tense, or angry, we are more likely to be more intense with our reactions. Dianne needs to incorporate an intervention or she might truly start to believe that she is indeed a bad parent.

Martha

Automatic Statements of the Perceived Outcome

"This is all your fault!"

"You are the reason our child will grow up without both parents."

"I hate what you have done to our family."

"I hope you are happy with your choice."

If you notice, all these statements include "you." This pragmatic approach speaks directly to the ego, which then influences how we feel about ourselves. This later becomes internalized by the receiving party and can eventually trigger negative cognitions and labels, such as, "It is all my fault." "I am a terrible person." "I shouldn't have done that."

Jerry

Automatic Statements of the Perceived Outcome

"I am a bad person."

"I shouldn't have done that."

"I don't deserve to be forgiven."

"I broke my partner's trust."

"I messed up."

Jerry is internalizing and labeling his process and is quickly creating a negative cycle that won't allow room for self-compassion or growth.

Leo

Automatic Statements of the Perceived Outcome

"Why couldn't it have been me?"

"Why did I survive?"

"I wish it had been me."

"I don't deserve to be alive."

"I could have done more."

One thing to consider when asking questions with a why–the thought implies that an answer exists to explain our situation. However, these thoughts don't always have an answer. Instead of promoting growth, it promotes stagnation and makes it almost impossible to move forward since you cannot reframe these thoughts. Leo cycles through his guilt for years with no intervention and his symptoms are increasing with time.

Rebecca

Automatic Statements of the Perceived Outcome

"I should have said yes."

"Now they'll think I am a bad friend."

Had she said yes, then some leading thoughts could be:

"Why can't I just say no?"

"I hate that I can't just hold my ground."

"I am betraying my feelings by going against something I don't want to do."

We often assume that our actions directly affect other people's feelings, and sometimes it is a factor in the perceived outcome.

Karen

Automatic Statements of the Perceived Outcome

Gaslight Guilt Statements:

"You don't have to do this."

"If you leave me, I won't know how to live my life without you."

"I will kill myself if you leave me."

Reactive Statements:

"If I break up with him, he's not going to be a good parent to our child."

"If he kills himself, I don't know how to live with that."

"It'll be my fault if he kills himself."

"He won't spend time with our child."

"I worry about his safety."

These types of statements are considered emotionally manipulative and his threats to hurt himself can be considered overkill. Overkill is when someone makes a comment that completely shifts the power and control that strays away from the original argument. If the argument was, "I think we should break up," but Kevin replies with "I will hurt myself if you leave me," it creates a dynamic where Karen now feels like she has no other options but to stay with Kevin for his safety.

Step Three: Feelings & Physical Sensations (Baseline)

In Step 2, I asked you to notice your body's physical sensations and emotions. This is called body scanning. **Body scanning** is practiced by closing the eyes, being in a comfortable position, and shifting the attention from the top of the head slowly down the body. Then notice whatever emotions might come about from thinking about the triggering event. Acknowledge the emotions but not dwell for too long, this process is only to recognize the feelings, and once written down, take three deep breaths and move on to the next step.

Initially, you might feel a sense of physical or emotional activation; remember these feelings are okay, and we want them to flow and know these are part of the natural emotional flow. Allow yourself to see it through. If the feelings are too intense, take a break.

When you're ready, begin body scanning. Close your eyes and notice the information that your body attempts to communicate with you without judgment.

Start by focusing your attention at the top of your head and slowly move the attention downward throughout your body to notice the physical sensations.

Note physical sensations such as tightness, tingling, tension, shakiness, changes in breathing, tearfulness, etc.

After you've gathered the physical information, take a moment to notice what feelings or emotions this event might bring up for you. Sometimes, you might have both positive and negative emotions, and it is all good information. Let the emotions flow.

Dianne
Feelings & Physical Sensations:

Guilt

Sad

Frustrated

Angry

Insecure

Defeated

Inadequate

Martha
Feelings & Physical Sensations:

Guilt

Sad

Tearful

Confused

Insecure

Self-doubt

Jerry

Feelings & Physical Sensations:

Regret

Guilt

Shame

Anxious

Tightness in the chest

Disappointment in self

Leo

Feelings & Physical Sensations:

Guilt

Sad

Anxious

Anger

Regret

Muscle Tension

Headache

Tightness in the chest

Tearful

Rebecca

Feelings & Physical Sensations:

Guilt

Insecure

Self-doubt

Anxious

Karen

Feelings & Physical Sensations:

Guilt

Anxious

Confused

Insecure

Self-doubt

Restless

Fidgety

Step Four: Activating Statement

To incorporate The Guilt Intervention, you must now identify the activating statement. This will help navigate through the noisy, unhelpful cycling of thoughts, questions, and intensifying emotions.

These automatic unfiltered thoughts will not disappear unless we reframe the statements and shift them into a rational perspective. To help process these automatic thoughts, identify and define them in one main statement; this is called the Activating Statement.

The activating statement structure should be specific and avoid general terms to help reduce overwhelming thoughts. The activating statement begins with an "I" statement that directly connects the triggering event and our perceived actions to the feelings of guilt. For example, "I feel guilty for..." or "I feel guilty because..." or "I feel guilty that..."

The most important thing to recognize is that The Guilt Intervention is not meant to justify, deny, or minimize the situation, but to help you grow from past behaviors and interactions.

Dianne

Activating statement:

"I feel guilty for yelling at my son and getting mad at him."

This guilt is Natural Guilt. With time, the symptoms diminish until they are activated again in a future interaction. Dianne does not feel guilty all the time, but it increases her feelings of inadequacy regarding her parenting. This can ultimately lead to feeling depressed.

Martha

Activating statement:

"I feel guilty for making the choice to divorce my partner, and now my child will grow up in a broken family."

This guilt is also Natural Guilt; however, this person's guilt had been reinforced by former partner's statements that solicited and forced feelings of Gaslight Guilt. These are very toxic and unhealthy statements that create an illusion of guilt, and it skews and deflects the accountability from one person to the other person, leaving Martha with all the responsibility of the perceived outcome.

Jerry

Activating statement:

"I regret cheating on my partner."

This type of guilt depends on how frequently the person holds on to the feelings of guilt—it could be a Natural or Toxic Guilt. For example, this person might feel bad initially but later be okay with the decision, or he could ruminate and hold the guilt in the form of subconscious self-punishment that will not allow him to forgive himself and move on. This self-inflicted punishment can be very difficult to break from if one refuses the self-compassion statement and continues to build feelings of regret.

The reality of this statement is this person did break their relationship trust and agreement of commitment. There is no justification, and this created mistrust and hurt. However, this doesn't mean this person couldn't hold themselves accountable, change, and grow from this experience.

Leo

Activating statement:

"I feel guilty for being alive when my friend died during the war."

Leo is experiencing existential or Survivor's Guilt. Leo cannot heal from the past due to holding on to the experience to uphold his friend's memory. Unfortunately, Leo's inability to grieve the loss has generalized into other main parts of his life and has affected other relationships. It has also triggered multiple flashbacks, nightmares, and other symptoms associated with post-traumatic stress.

(Due to graphic experience, certain details will be omitted.)

Rebecca

Activating statement:

"I feel guilty for saying no to my friend when they asked for help with getting a ride home."

This is Natural Guilt and typically resolves itself relatively fast. However, Rebecca's insecurity and fear of saying no to people have compiled over time. The complication comes from the internal dissonance happening between the person's decision to say no and the emotional weight attached to a deeper value or belief system. This particular person said no and her internal struggle would be that she now feels guilty for saying no and had self-critical statements such as, "I hurt their feelings," "They won't want to be my friend anymore," or "I am a bad friend."

However, if she would have said yes, she could have struggled with feeling like she betrayed herself and her own needs. Typically, people who struggle to say no derive from passive personality, introverted behavior, or people-pleasing, all of which can be attributed to a core value or personality that influences how they make these choices.

Karen

Activating statement:

"I feel guilty for wanting to end my relationship, but I also worry about his feelings."

The original idea would be considered Natural Guilt; however, similar to Martha, Karen's current partner is making statements developing Gaslight Guilt. Karen is struggling to move forward with her life and feels very confused because Kevin's statements are creating an emotional imbalance flooding Karen with negative feelings and inability to think clearly about what she wants to do regarding her relationship. This is typically a red flag to consider. If your partner is creating self-doubt, confusion, displacing, or projecting his or her insecurities onto you, this is a toxic and unhealthy relationship. It may be good to reach out to a professional to help create an emotionally safe environment to process and explore those feelings.

Whether guilt is real or perceived, how does one practice self-forgiveness and break the cycle of guilt?

Which of these scenarios do you relate to or have experienced?

Do you have a triggering event and if so, what would be your activating statement?

Exercise:

Depending on the category of guilt, you might have a different intensity of responses. Practice self-regulation and it is okay to take a break. To help you get started, first sit back and allow your mind to float and identify a person or interaction that feels the strongest to you. If there are multiple interactions from a specific person, rank them from strongest to least intensity. For The Process to be effective, be specific to each triggering event. Remember, sometimes, there might be feelings of depression, anxiety, or anger that could be masking the feelings of guilt, so explore any triggering event that creates any "should" statements.

If the most intense event feels too overwhelming, you can start with a smaller event. Once you get used to The Process, challenge yourself to tackle a more intense triggering event. Remember, you can read through the whole book first and then come back to this section.

Exercise:
Current Steps:

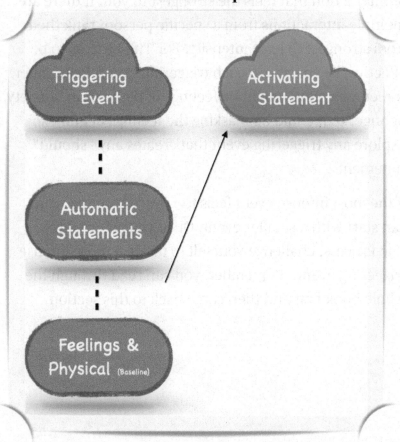

Step One-Triggering Event:

Helpful Questions:

What was the event that created feelings of guilt?

_____

_____

_____

_____

_____

_____

_____

Check to see if you also feel shame

Only focus on the behavioral guilt vs belief of shame

Step Two- Automatic Statements of Perceived Outcome:

Helpful Questions:

What are you telling yourself about the triggering event?

How do you perceive your actions?

What are the "should" statements?

_____

_____

_____

_____

_____

_____

_____

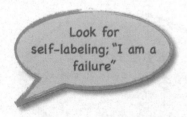

Look for self-labeling; "I am a failure"

Step Three-Feelings & Physical Sensations: Baseline

Helpful Questions:

What emotions do you notice when you think about this?

What physical sensations are coming up for you?

_____

_____

_____

_____

_____

_____

_____

Emotions:
sad, mad, anxious, guilt,
etc.

Sensations:
Pain, tension, tingling,
tightness, etc.

Step Four - Activating Statement:

Helpful Questions:

What is the main thought that is making you feel guilty?

What is the most frequent thought that keeps coming up?

Structure of statement:

"I feel guilty for, I feel guilty because, I feel guilty that...etc. (*perceived outcome*)"

_____

_____

_____

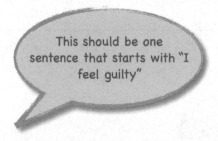

This should be one sentence that starts with "I feel guilty"

-

Take a moment to take three deep breaths and take a break if you need to regulate. Finish The Process to break the cycle.

You are doing great!

Chapter 3
Accountability

Accountability is a state in which we hold ourselves or others responsible for actions that occurred. Self-accountability will lead to an empowering level of growth and transform how we perceive our behaviors. There may be barriers that hinder us from seeing our self-accountability, or we may have challenges seeing what others may be accountable for.

For example, you made a statement that hurt your partner: "You are a terrible person because you never listen to me." You may feel justified and the belief is, "He deserved it because I'm always asking him to listen." The statement might be true, yet the comment of "terrible person" or even the yelling or hostile tone would be within our self-accountability, and not listening would fall under the other person's accountability. Therefore, when exploring accountability, you will find there are responsibilities true of both parties.

Have you ever cycled through a memory, situation, or a thought that creates feelings of guilt? How long before you can recognize, let go of, forgive, or accept the situation so it allows you to feel closure, freedom, or even empowerment? For some people, the feeling of guilt is created by cycling thoughts and does not allow for movement, growth, or energy flow.

Accepting our behaviors,
positive or negative,
is the first step to accountability.

Accountability allows us awareness of our behaviors and that of others. This first statement of accountability establishes a logical and rational perspective on how we view the situation. This helps isolate the logical and emotional components, so the feelings of guilt or other negative feelings don't influence our perspective.

It is very important to view these statements as facts instead of internalizing them as feelings. These accountability statements are not intended to justify or minimize your actions or other's actions, but to see them for what they are. These statements are to realign the perspective of accountability and accurately assign accountability where it belongs and not be emotionally skewed towards one person. We fail to let go of guilt because for some, this is as far as processing the cycling thought goes, creating the guilt of our actions but not flowing into a place of change or self-growth.

Start by assessing the motive of your choice without judgment, and the behaviors or the facts that occurred during the triggering event.

Dianne

Activating statement:

"I feel guilty for yelling at my son and getting mad at him."

Accountability statement:

What are the facts or actual behaviors that happened?

During this section, we will compile a list of the factual behaviors that occurred.

"My son wanted to keep playing outside."

"It was raining."

"I yelled at him because he wasn't listening and I didn't want him to get sick."

"I chased him and had to force him inside."

"He cried afterward."

What am I accountable for?

> *"I am accountable for yelling at him."*

> *"I am accountable for grabbing him intently."*

> *"I am accountable for asking him nicely the first time."*

Second step is the other party's accountability (if applicable):

What are you not accountable for?

"I am not accountable for my son not wanting to come inside."

> *"I am not accountable for my son ignoring me."*

> *"I am not accountable for him running away from me."*

Dianne tried to communicate her needs calmly, but unfortunately, her son did not want to follow the instructions. Her son was not being compliant and perhaps in need of discipline, but it does not justify the parent's reactions. Dianne did yell and grabbed him in an intense manner—no marks were left, but this speaks to the frustration that parents can often feel. We will explore how to navigate through this.

Martha

Activating statement:

"I feel guilty for making the choice to divorce my partner, and now my child will grow up in a broken family."

Accountability statement:

What are the facts or actual behaviors that happened?

"I made the decision to get a divorce."

"I made the decision that was best for my child and me."

"I was respectful throughout my interactions and did the best I could to make the separation easy by staying calm."

"I was unhappy in the marriage and decided to move away from an unhealthy relationship."

"I took emotional responsibility for myself."

What am I accountable for?

"I am accountable for making the choice to divorce and being respectful."

The second step is the other party's accountability (if applicable):

What are you not accountable for?

"I am not accountable for my partner's abusive behavior towards me."

"I am not accountable for other people's feelings regarding my decision."

"I am not accountable for the relationship between my son and his father."

"I am not emotionally responsible for my ex-husband's lack of coping or self-care."

Martha was feeling intense guilt because of displaced guilt that had been distorted and was disproportionate to her actions. We now have a clear perspective on who is accountable for what, and this section is strictly rational and logical, which focuses on using the left-brain function.

Jerry

Activating statement:

"I feel guilty for cheating on my partner."

Accountability statement:

What are the facts or actual behaviors that happened?

"I made the decision to be unfaithful."

"I lied to my partner."

"I had sexual relations with someone else."

"I initiated or participated in interactions that led up to the sexual affair."

The reality here is that Jerry is accountable for all of his negative actions and did make decisions that affected the relationship. There is no denying or justifying the facts. This can be hard to acknowledge, but doing so would avoid accountability. This may hinder your healing development and you may find yourself in persecutory guilt, which doesn't allow for a healthy flow of emotions. If Jerry is resistant to acknowledging a self-compassion statement, a forgiveness blockage might need to be addressed and explored first.

What am I accountable for?

"I am accountable for having an affair and breaking my partner's trust."

Leo

Activating statement:

"I feel guilty for being alive when my friend died during the war."

Accountability statement:

What are the facts or actual behaviors that happened?

"I chose to follow orders that were given to me."

"I made the choice to be in the military."

"I froze."

What am I accountable for?

"I am accountable for making an effort to revive my friend."

The second step is the other party's accountability (if applicable):

What are you not accountable for?

"I am not accountable for my friend dying."

"I am not accountable for the attack."

"I am not accountable for freezing at first due to the autonomic nervous system."

This situation is different; most people who struggle with Survivor's Guilt struggle with the idea that they could have done more. This might be challenging if the person refuses to let go of the belief there was more they could have done. In retrospect, we can always do more, but this also develops an introspective pressure that no longer allows room for mistakes and can develop resistance or rejection towards the self-compassion statement. It creates feelings of undeserved relief of guilt or undeserving of self-forgiveness. Leo's freezing in the moment creates the illusion he was at fault; however, his reaction stems from an autonomous internal reaction from the brain and nervous system he had no initial control over.

Rebecca

Activating statement:

"I feel guilty for saying no to my friend when they asked for help with getting a ride home."

Accountability statement:

What are the facts or actual behaviors that happened?

"I made the decision to say no."

"I said no to something I didn't feel comfortable doing."

What am I accountable for?

"I am accountable for making the choice to say yes or no."

The second step is the other party's accountability (if applicable):

What are you not accountable for?

> *"I am not accountable for my friend being out."*

> *"I am not accountable for my friend finding a ride home."*

Rebecca held her ground but later felt Natural Guilt for saying no and allowed the statements to flood, leaving an overwhelming feeling of guilt. After processing the accountability statements, Rebecca felt emotional release and the feelings of self-doubt and insecurity vanished.

Karen

Activating statement:

> *"I feel guilty for wanting to end my relationship, but I also worry about his feelings."*

Accountability statement:

What are the facts or actual behaviors that happened or are happening?

> *"I feel unhappy in the relationship."*

> *"I worry about my partner's emotional wellness."*

> *"I worry about my partner's physical safety."*

> *"I am unsure if I want to stay or leave the relationship."*

> *"I worry about the challenges of co-parenting if we separate."*

What am I accountable for?

"I am accountable for my feelings and the decision I make, whether it is to stay or leave the relationship."

The second step is the other party's accountability (if applicable):

What are you not accountable for?

"I am not accountable for my partner's emotional challenges."

"I am not accountable for my partner's unstable comments of overkill."

"I am not accountable for the relationship between my son and his father."

"I am not accountable for my partner's lack of coping or self-care."

Karen is struggling to make her decision and the goal here is not to provide her with an answer, but to provide clarity by removing the overwhelmingly imbalanced emotions and guilt to help her feel emotionally safe to logically decide for her well-being.

Exercise:
Current Steps:

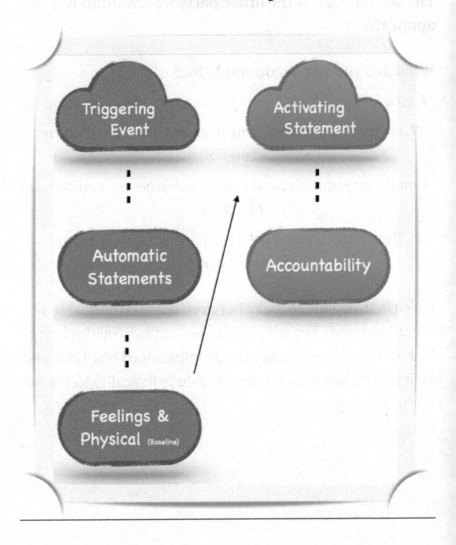

Accountability

Helpful Questions:

What is the behavior you are displaying at the moment?

What did you say and how did you say it?

How did you respond?

Was it positive or negative?

Did you cross any boundaries?

Were you aggressive in any way?

Were you assertive and respectful?

What actions did you take?

During this section, we will compile a list of factual behaviors within your control.

Step Five - Accountability Statements:

Structure of statement:

What are the facts or actual behaviors that happened?

_____

_____

_____

Focus on facts and avoid assumptions

"I am accountable for..."

_____

_____

_____

_____

> Focus on your
> actions only

Second part - the other party's accountability _(if applicable)_:

Structure of statement:

"I am not accountable for..."

_____

_____

_____

_____

> Focus on
> the other person's
> actions

Chapter 4
Self-Compassion & Affirmations

You are not perfect and that is okay. Being imperfect does not mean that you are a bad person. To the contrary–accepting this premise may increase the welcoming of self-compassion, whereas perceiving yourself as perfect may create some challenges. It can create an illusion that nothing you do ever is wrong and could be perceived as a sense of denial or deflection. Being "perfect" doesn't leave room for errors and most importantly, it doesn't leave room for self-compassion.

Self-compassion is a state in which we allow kindness to ourselves. This can be in positive affirmations, such as "I am doing the best I can," or "I am a kind individual," but overall, it provides a sense of internal patience and empathetic validation. It can be hard for some to allow self-compassion, but we are hindering our own healing without it.

*Strive to become a great person;
it's only when we strive to
become a perfect person that we
face the fallacies of life.*

The truth is we all fail, wrong someone, make mistakes, or simply just mess up. Yet, the story doesn't have to end there.

Through self-compassion statements, we accept that we are not perfect and have room for growth, creating a sense of flow that will move us away from stagnation.

We will explore two types of statements: self-compassion and affirmations. Self-compassion will focus on statements that promote being kind, loving, patient, and supportive. Affirmations will focus on statements that promote encouragement, growth, positivity, motivation and empowerment.

Self-compassion statements are used for negative accountability statements, and affirmations are for positive accountability statements. They are both meant to support growth and empower yourself.

When exploring self-compassion, one thing to consider is that this statement is not meant to justify an action, like saying, "It is okay that I yelled, because that person deserved it." The self-compassion statement should be not directly associated with the accountability statement but more general towards the self. For example, a general accountability statement sounds like, "It's okay to feel dysregulated sometimes, but I am working on myself." A good rule of thumb is to say something that you would tell a loved one if they were in a similar situation.

Structure this statement with a comment that feels authentic. The self-compassion statement should be accurate and genuine and feels right to you; otherwise, it won't have a very strong effect. The self-compassion statement is the first act of emotional defense against the negative feelings of guilt. Once you have crafted the self-compassion statement, ask yourself, "Do I truly accept these statements?" "Is this authentic?"

To truly love yourself is to be kind and compassionate.

Dianne

Activating statement:

"I feel guilty for yelling at my son and getting mad at him."

Accountability statement:

"I am accountable for yelling at him."

"I am accountable for grabbing him intensely."

"I am accountable for asking him nicely the first time."

Self-Compassion statement:

"Being a parent can be difficult."

"I am doing the best I can as a parent."

"I do love my son."

Dianne saw that one negative response does not make her a bad parent. She was quick to judge herself but neglected to see some of the positive experiences with her son. She also gave herself grace by recognizing that being a parent can indeed be challenging and we don't always have the right answers or responses.

Martha

Activating statement:

"I feel guilty for making the choice to divorce my partner, and now my child will grow up in a broken family."

Accountability statement:

"I am accountable for making the choice to divorce and was respectful."

Self-Affirmation statement:

"I know I made the best decision for my child and myself."

Martha is now feeling the shift in emotional weight, but more importantly, she recognizes that her rights and freedom of choice are supported by her self-compassion statement. She regained her trust in her ability to make the right decision for her and her child.

Jerry

Activating statement:

"I feel guilty for cheating on my partner."

Accountability statement:

"I am accountable for having an affair and breaking my partner's trust."

Self-Compassion statement:

"I made a mistake; I am not perfect."

Jerry has already recognized his mistake, and for this section, we want to avoid comments that include accountability. This is another pragmatic process to look for and reframe thoughts. Self-compassion should not be conditional, so it has to be a stand-alone statement. Unlike with other types of guilt, we want to have this statement to provide emotional relief and should avoid statements such as, *"I made a mistake, and recognize the hurt I caused, but I am human, and I am not perfect."* Also, avoid statements such as *"I am not perfect and could have done better."*

Whenever we use the word "but" in a sentence, we are negating the first part of the statement, so the self-compassion statement should be one sentence without the word "but" in it. Structure this statement by speaking to the hurt ego of the self, start with "I."

Leo

Activating statement:

"I feel guilty for being alive when my friend died during the war."

Accountability statement:

"I am accountable for not doing enough."

Self-Compassion & Affirmation Statement:

"I know there was nothing else I could have done, and it is not my fault my friend died."

Leo struggled to come up with this statement but eventually did accept this as his self-compassion statement. Leo had to explore the concept of grief and recognize that letting go of the incident does not mean letting go of his friend. Leo also had to explore cognitive distortions blocking the authenticity of this statement.

This shows there are different levels of intensity of guilt, but also that if you are struggling to accept the statements listed, that is a sign of a deeper concept or belief that might be blocking or making it challenging to achieve a place of healing.

This also demonstrates that guilt can be very complex, and reach out to a mental health professional if you feel like you cannot move past this point on your own.

Rebecca

Activating statement:

"I feel guilty for saying no to my friend when they asked for help with getting a ride home."

Accountability statement:

"I am accountable for making the choice to say yes or no."

Self-Compassion & Affirmation Statement:

"I have the right to say no and feel secure about my choices."

Rebecca's statement supports her accountability statement, and she instantly feels the power to choose. This statement completely cancels all self-doubt and insecurity. She regained confidence and control of her choices by refocusing the attention to her right of choice and not on other people's feelings.

Karen

Activating statement:

"I feel guilty for wanting to end my relationship, but I also worry about his feelings."

Accountability statement:

"I am accountable for my feelings and whatever decision I make, whether it is to stay or leave the relationship."

Self-Compassion & Affirmation Statement:

"I am unsure of what the future might bring, and that is okay."

Karen's intensity of manipulative guilt has now been reduced to Natural Guilt. Even though she is still unsure of the future, she can now think clearly and create emotional space to explore and continue to contemplate her future decision, with no emotional manipulation.

Exercise:

Current Steps:

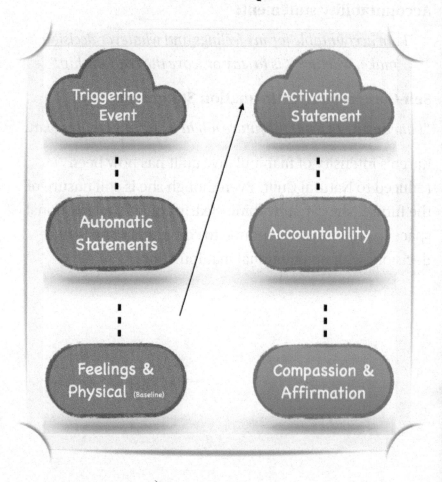

Self-Compassion & Affirmations

Step Six: Self-Compassion & Affirmation Statement

Helpful Questions:

What would you tell someone in a similar situation?

How would you show empathy towards someone else?

What would you like to tell your past self?

Structure this statement by emphasizing the pragmatic approach. For example, instead of saying "I think I made the right choice," use "I know I made the right choice." This removes the self-doubt and replaces it with a confident statement.

In addition, the statements should focus on something that you believe about yourself. For example, "I am a kind person." Explore past scenarios where you've demonstrated behaviors that support this statement. These statements should be crafted as a fact.

What is the difference between self-compassion and affirmation? A self-compassion statement will typically feel loving, supportive, empathetic, validating, compassionate, kind, and caring. An affirmation statement will encourage, motivate, inspire, support, and empower.

What are your Self-Compassion & Affirmation Statements?

Self-Compassion Statements:

_____

_____

_____

> Does it feel authentic?

Affirmation Statements:

_____

_____

_____

> Do you accept these statements?

Chapter 5
Awareness

Awareness is defined by the level of knowledge and understanding of the information that exists, whether internal or external. Internal awareness includes having insight into our inner world, the way we feel, our behaviors, the context of our thoughts and, on a deeper analytical level, the process of how we think, including our own cognitive distortions. External awareness includes acknowledging and understanding our exterior environment and outside world, including factors such as the situation itself, other people involved, and developing circumstances.

The awareness statement serves two purposes; the first is to help identify the factors we have no control over and the second is to increase our awareness of our internal and external triggers. A trigger is a stressor that can influence an emotional response--an automatic thought or a physical or behavioral reaction. This is why The Process shifts back and forth from logical-self and rational thinking while consciously reinforcing and supporting the emotional self.

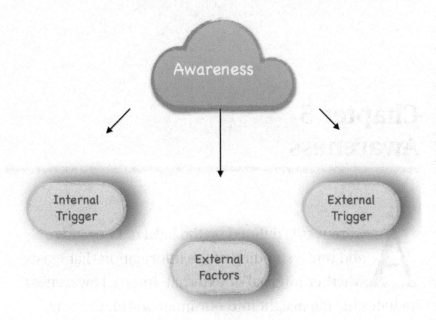

Internal triggers include a thought, feeling, or even physical sensation. An example of an automatic negative or intrusive thought could be, "I don't like the way my body looks." Another example of an internal trigger is waking up feeling sad. Examples of physical sensations are tightness in the chest, tingling, pain, or other somatic complaints and tension.

External triggers include events, people, places, or things associated with a negative experience we have had or connections to a belief system we are hyper-vigilant about.

For example, meeting someone who reminds you of a middle school bully that just gives you a bad vibe. It could be visiting a street where you've had a bad experience, such as a car accident.

It is helpful to have an awareness of your triggers. It helps you understand what is influencing your feelings or reactions. It can also ease the mind by recognizing there is a cause and effect happening, and that you're not just spiraling for no reason. There is peace in knowing why you feel or do what you do.

Step Seven: Awareness

Dianne

Activating statement:

"*I feel guilty for yelling at my son and getting mad at him.*"

Accountability statement:

"*I am accountable for yelling at him.*"

"*I am accountable for grabbing him intensely.*"

"*I am accountable for asking him nicely the first time.*"

Self-Compassion statement:

"*Being a parent can be difficult.*"

"*I am doing the best I can as a parent.*"

"*I do love my son.*"

Awareness statements:

"*It was raining, and children could get sick if they stay in wet clothes for too long.*"

"Children don't understand that getting mud in the house is not always fun for the person who has to clean it up."

"Asking someone repeatedly for the same thing can increase frustration and tension."

"Running in the rain can make someone slip and get hurt."

"Children who don't listen can increase frustration."

Dianne understands the external factor of the rain influenced her response due to creating a sense of urgency. Dianne wanted to prevent her son from potentially getting hurt or sick and she knew if she ran out there, she would also get wet and then she would need to change or shower, and these are all extra tasks she didn't have the energy for. Dianne also understands that her son saying "no" is a trigger for her, so she will also focus on incorporating a process to help her cope with those triggers.

Martha

Activating statement:

"I feel guilty for making the choice to divorce my partner, and now my child will grow in a broken family."

Accountability statement:

"I am accountable for making the choice to divorce and was respectful throughout the process."

Self-Compassion & Affirmation Statement:

"I know I made the best decision for my child and myself."

Awareness statements:

"Getting married at a young age can be difficult."

"Being in a toxic abusive relationship is unhealthy."

"There were red flags that were hard to identify."

Martha realizes that she made the correct decision and has power over the situation to let go of the guilt. At some point, we have to make the conscious effort to shift from the victim mentality to empowerment, and it starts by taking emotional responsibility for our actions and not the past version of ourselves.

Jerry

Activating statement:

"I feel guilty for cheating on my partner."

Accountability statement:

"I am accountable for having an affair and breaking my partner's trust."

Self-Compassion & Affirmation Statement:

"I made a mistake; I am not perfect."

Awareness statements:

"There was alcohol involved."

"This was a co-worker and there were constant interactions."

"There was a conference happening."

Jerry had no control over who attended the event, and it appears the two individuals had slowly built various levels of connection leading to an affair. Again, this is not a justification, nor should it be taken away from the accountability statement. Instead, it should be an awareness of the factors that influenced and facilitated his decision.

This statement also serves as self-awareness of what your triggers might be. Knowing your internal and external triggers could help influence your choices and know which people, places, or things to be mindful and perhaps cautious about in the future.

Leo

Activating statement:

"I feel guilty for being alive when my friend died during the war."

Accountability statement:

"I am accountable for not doing enough."

Self-Compassion statement:

"I know there was nothing else I could have done, and it is not my fault my friend died."

Awareness statements:

"There was a war happening."

"There were orders to attend that particular area."

"Nobody could have expected that the attack would happen at that particular place and time."

"Military training includes the importance of repressing emotions."

Leo holds on to a lot that has nothing to do with his accountability or that was within his level of control. This awareness statement supports the self-compassion statement and begins to logically support and reinforce the positive emotional aspect of compassion.

It increases his understanding he is not 100% to blame for the loss; it increases the understanding he had little to no control and allows room for self-compassion.

Rebecca

Activating statement:

"I feel guilty for saying no to my friend when they asked for help with getting a ride home."

Accountability statement:

"I am accountable for making the choice to say yes or no."

Self-Compassion & Affirmation Statement:

"I have the right to say no and feel secure about my choices."

Awareness statement:

"There was an event that my friend attended."

"Work was very difficult that day."

"It was very late, and it was bedtime."

Rebecca realizes that she was struggling with her internal distress from having a difficult day and it did influence her decision to say no. Again, this statement helps support the self-compassion statement from a logical perspective.

Sometimes, we feel overwhelmed by the activating statement, and we fail to step back and notice the additional factors that influence a decision. Rebecca remembered that she is entitled to just say no and need not justify or rationale for her choices.

Karen

Activating statement:

"I feel guilty for wanting to end my relationship, but I also worry about his feelings."

Accountability statement:

"I am accountable for my feelings and whatever decision I make, whether is to stay or leave the relationship."

Self-Compassion & Affirmation Statement:

"I am unsure of what the future might, bring, and that is okay."

Awareness statements:

"Breakups can cause financial concerns."

"There are housing and living situations that are uncertain."

"It is unsure how children can feel from separating parents."

"Breakups can make someone feel uncertain regarding co-parenting."

Karen continues to find herself in a place of limbo and is now recognizing additional factors to consider that could affect her future decisions. Karen had to explore problem-solving techniques to help facilitate the movement from her "stuck" place and where she wanted to be regarding her situation.

Remember, if we stay in a situation we are not happy about, it creates a lack of emotional flow, leading to symptoms of depression or anxiety.

Exercise:
Current Steps:

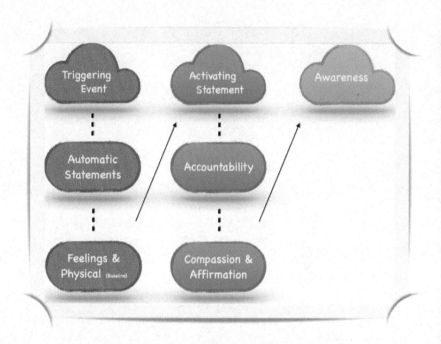

Awareness

Helpful Questions:

What are the external factors at play?

What else influenced the situation?

What was happening outside of your control?

Was anyone or anything else indirectly involved?

Structure this as a list of statements or of other factual circumstances happening that you may or may not have control over in the present moment. It is also important to avoid "I" statements and generalize the statement from a third-person view. Unlike other statements, since we have no control over the external factors, it is important to pragmatically remove yourself or any other party from this statement and reframe it to a general concept.

For example, instead of saying: "I got married at a young age and I didn't know any better," reframe it to: "Getting married at a young age can be difficult." Another example could be: "My baby was sick," to "It is difficult to understand the needs of a sick baby."

What are your Awareness statements?

Structure of Statements:

Avoid pronouns such as "I, he/she, them, they" and use general statements.

Awareness Statements:

External Factors:

_____

_____

_____

Remember, these are things outside of your control

Internal & External Triggers:

_____

_____

_____

Your personal reactions to thoughts, places, people, situations

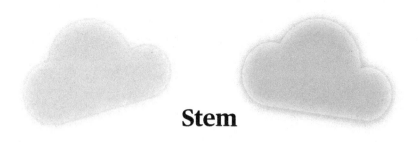

Stem

A drip of blood smears on the floor, something that I hadn't seen before.

Where did it come from, I look up to the sky, no sign of where this drop had dropped, the color red was bright.

I look back and I see a trail of red, I hadn't noticed, is this what I'm leaving behind, could it be what I'm holding on tight.

My grip, I feel no pain all I had left was a stem.

My hand feels numb and the thorns were stuck penetrating my skin and now I can see. This is where the blood released.

I don't feel the pain I'm shocked, this is now a stem, I held on too long and too tight, for what this once was is now gone out of sight.

It was beautiful, it was very full, it was love for me and I thought It was protecting me, it's hard to see, but now I see, that now I'm free.

I'll put this stem down, I'll wash my hand now.

I'll look again and find myself another stem but this time I'll keep it close...... I'll find myself another ROSE.

Chapter 6
Self-Growth

Growth starts from within-- it is up to you to make the change happen. Holding on to an emotion, a situation, or a memory that no longer serves a purpose and only feels painful is like holding on to the stem of a rose that has only thorns left. It creates a feeling of stagnation that can lead to depression. This concept can be applied to anything you might be holding on to that feels painful. This final step in The Process is where you make the conscious effort to change, to be accountable, to be emotionally responsible for your feelings, and overall, to grow from this moment forward.

The goal of self-growth is to reduce the repetition or cycling of triggering events or thoughts that can induce guilt. This is one of the most important steps because this is the action step that breaks the emotional stagnation. By agreeing with yourself, you are taking the next step to follow through with the original concept of accountability.

This section helps counter the "should have" statements by shifting from the past "could haves" to the present "will do's." This is another pragmatic approach that helps break from the past and the ruminating thoughts while influencing a positive emotional flow.

Finally, meet yourself where you are. You may be ready to take action, or maybe just contemplate action. It's important to be realistic on what changes you will make. Sometimes, if you are struggling with Survivor's Guilt, it may be important to also incorporate processing of the grief and loss. Remember, when dealing with grief and loss, it may take time to heal, but The Process can provide you with a good place to begin. Also, if you find yourself blocked by a belief system, it's okay to incorporate additional work with a mental health professional. Sometimes it is helpful to make smaller, more attainable goals to break this step down and to make it feel less overwhelming.

Dianne

Activating statement:

"I feel guilty for yelling at my son and getting mad at him."

Accountability statement:

"I am accountable for yelling at him."

"I am accountable for grabbing him intensely."

"I am accountable for asking him nicely the first time."

Self-Compassion statement:

"Being a parent can be difficult."

"I am doing the best I can as a parent."

"I do love my son."

Awareness statements:

"It was raining, and children could get sick if they stay in wet clothes for too long."

"Children don't understand that getting mud in the house is not always fun for the person who has to clean it up."

"Asking someone repeatedly for the same thing can increase frustration and tension."

"Running in the rain can make someone slip and get hurt."

"Children who don't listen can increase frustration."

Self-growth agreements:

"I will work with my son to understand what could happen when someone is out in the rain."

"I am going to reinforce healthy boundaries for my son to understand when saying 'no' is appropriate versus defiant."

"I will explore ways to regulate my frustrations prior to disciplining my son."

"I will continue to give myself positive affirmations to stay confident about my parenting."

Dianne's growth statements are positively focused on her not only working with her son but also on herself. She realized she was internalizing her frustrations and then displacing them on her son.

After completing the Process, Dianne reported feeling confident in her parenting and realized that being frustrated or snapping at her kid does not negate that she is a loving and caring parent. She realized those two experiences can coexist-- you could have a bad day and still be a wonderful parent.

Dianne has a great relationship with her son and even though she will continue to feel frustrated because let's face it, kids will be kids, and she might be snappy, she no longer believes this makes her a bad parent.

Martha

Activating statement:

"I feel guilty for making the choice to divorce my partner, and now my child will grow in a broken family."

Accountability statement:

"I am accountable for making the choice to divorce and was respectful throughout the process."

Self-Compassion & Affirmation Statement:

"I know I made the best decision for my child and myself."

Awareness statements:

"Getting married at a young age can be difficult."

"Being in a toxic abusive relationship is unhealthy."

"There were red flags that were hard to identify."

Self-growth agreements:

> *"I will teach my son coping skills and love him."*
>
> *"I am going to work on myself."*
>
> *"I will learn what abusive behaviors are and learn to avoid them."*
>
> *"I will learn how to read red flags."*
>
> *"I will do my best to co-parent."*
>
> *"I will not let my ex-husband's lack of relationship with my son influence my feelings."*

Martha's growth statements are correlated to the original thoughts creating the feelings of anxiety and guilt. After applying a new perspective by reframing her thoughts, her feelings also adjusted, and she finished it with action steps to push past the negative feelings.

Martha reported feeling empowered and is now happy with her decision. She continues to work on herself, and her child is adapting quickly to the separation. She is now focusing on her own healing journey and owning her happiness.

Jerry

Activating statement:

> *"I feel guilty for cheating on my partner."*

Accountability statement:

"I am accountable for having an affair and breaking my partner's trust."

Self-Compassion & Affirmation Statement:

"I made a mistake; I am not perfect."

Awareness statements:

"There was alcohol involved."

"This was a co-worker and there were constant interactions."

"There was a conference happening."

Self-growth agreements:

"I will work on rebuilding trust with my partner."

"I am going to learn how to navigate through my external triggers."

"I will set healthy boundaries with people."

"I will set healthy internal boundaries with myself."

"I will not put myself in situations that are triggering for me."

"I will be honest and transparent with my partner."

Jerry and his partner continue to focus on their relationship and have found the power of honesty and consistent behavior. Jerry and his partner are now engaged and owning their happiness.

Leo

Activating statement:

"I feel guilty for being alive when my friend died during the war."

Accountability statement:

"I am accountable for not doing enough."

Self-Compassion statement:

"I know there was nothing else I could have done, and it is not my fault my friend died."

Awareness statements:

"There was a war happening."

"There were orders to attend that particular area."

"Nobody could have expected that the attack would happen at that particular place and time."

"Military training includes the importance of repressing emotions."

Self-Compassion & Affirmation Statement:

"I will work on processing my grief."

"I am going to allow myself to practice self-forgiveness."

"I am going to be open to the feedback I am given to help me during my healing process."

"I will not blame myself for what happened."

"I will focus on rebuilding relationships."

"I will work on being emotionally responsible for my feelings and actions."

Leo continues to work on his healing journey and is actively doing trauma work. Leo did report that his nightmares stopped and he no longer feels guilty for what happened. Leo is now working on rebuilding his relationships and exploring new ways to find joy in his life. Leo is working on owning his happiness.

Rebecca

Activating statement:

"I feel guilty for saying no to my friend when they asked for help with getting a ride home."

Accountability statement:

"I am accountable for making the choice to say yes or no."

Self-Compassion & Affirmation Statement:

"I have the right to say no and feel secure about my choices."

Awareness statement:

"There was an event that my friend attended."

"Work was very difficult that day."

"It was very late, and it was bedtime."

Self-growth agreements:

"I will continue to practice being assertive."

"I am going practice holding my ground and being true to myself."

"I will not allow myself to feel guilty for saying no."

Rebecca has identified a new value system and through additional coaching, she is now a very confident and assertive individual that no longer feels bad for saying no. She lost no friends and is owning her happiness.

Karen

Activating statement:

"I feel guilty for wanting to end my relationship, but I also worry about his feelings."

Accountability statement:

"I am accountable for my feelings and whatever decision I make, whether is to stay or leave the relationship."

Self-Compassion & Affirmation Statement:

"I am unsure of what the future might bring, and that is okay."

Awareness statements:

"Breakups can cause financial concerns."

"There are housing and living situations that are uncertain."

"It is unsure how children can feel from separating parents."

"Breakups can make someone feel uncertain regarding co-parenting."

Self-Growth Agreements:

"I will be kind to myself during this decision-making process."

"I am going to take time to process and think about my situation."

"I am going explore all of my options."

"I will not allow myself to be mentally or emotionally manipulated into making a decision."

"I will practice self-care and explore healthy boundaries for my relationship."

Karen decided on separating and her adjustment was challenging. However, she has no regrets or guilt for making the decision. She continues to work on herself and is still healing from the past but is currently working on owning her happiness.

Exercise:
Current Steps:

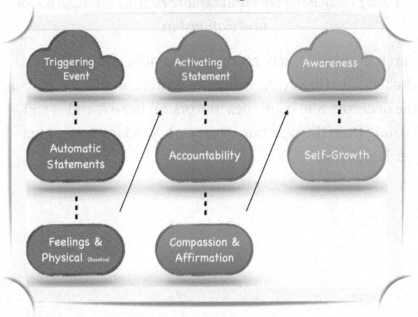

Step Eight: Self-Growth Agreements

Helpful Questions:

What have you learned from the experience?

What have you learned about yourself?

What are you willing to do differently?

How can you change moving forward?

Structure this statement by starting with "I will...", "I am going to..." or "I can..." The final shift is a combination incorporating the logical and emotional self with emotional empowerment and rational statements. This will launch you into being an empowered and confident individual by finalizing your new level of control and power.

The Self-Growth Agreements also should be directly associated with your accountability statement. Self-growth supports and builds confidence in your decisions. These are intended to be agreements that are action-based and realistic.

What are your Self-growth Agreements?

Structure of Statements:

    "I will..." "I am going to..." "I can..."

Self-growth agreements:

_____

_____

_____

_____

_____

_____

_____

Are they attainable, realistic, specific to the triggering event?

Step Nine: Feelings & Physical Sensations: Shifted

After completing your Self-Growth Agreements, let's see how your new perspective feels. Take a moment to notice what emotions or new sensations you might have.

Re-read your activating statement and observe the changes.

Helpful Questions:

What do you notice when you think about the activating statement?

Is it still triggering?

What do you notice in your body?

Are you still feeling the same emotions?

Does the statement make sense, or does it no longer apply?

Do you want to reframe it to something else?

Finish this section by giving yourself a 20-second hug while focusing on your new perspective and motivation.

Exercise:

What are your Feelings & Physical Sensations?

Activating statement:

_____

_____

Accountability Statement:

_____

_____

Self-Compassion & Affirmation Statement:

_____

_____

_____

Awareness Statements:

_____

_____

_____

_____

Self-growth agreements:

_____

_____

_____

_____

_____

_____

_____

Feelings & Physical Sensations: Shifted

_____

_____

_____

_____

_____

Chapter 7
Kind Words

You did it, you beautiful human! You pushed yourself through the hardest part of emotional stagnation. You allowed yourself to feel and heal and reframe your experience to find emotional freedom. Remember, if you experienced barriers to letting go, explore what self-forgiveness means to you and remember no one is perfect.

Now that you have mastered The Process, this will be your intervention and healthy defense mechanism for any potential triggering events.

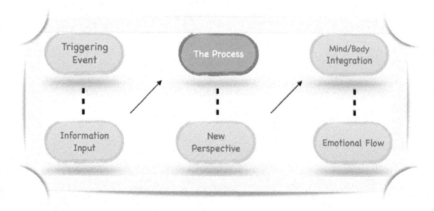

In the chart on the previous page, you will notice that The Process bypasses the defense mechanisms, helps to increase emotional flow, and aids in preventing emotional stagnation.

The end result is that you stay grounded, regulated, and can shield any unhealthy guilt IN... THE... MOMENT! Isn't that amazing!

Thank you for doing The Process and allowing yourself to become empowered. Treat yourself well, and remember only you have the power to change your world and truly own your happiness!

Forgiveness is permission to let go.

Oh! I almost forgot. Frank the fisherman went back to the market and met with the other fisherman one more time. Frank was ready to learn. He asked good questions, and he was open to the knowledge and feedback the other fisherman offered.

Frank updated his tackle box and, feeling confident to take on a new challenge, and he walked right over that hill. Frank set out his tools, made the adjustments, cast his rod, and through the glimmering water, there it was! Frank the fisherman caught the biggest fish he'd ever laid eyes upon. The fish jumped right out of the water almost instantly. Frank walked home proudly that day. That night, he feasted with his happy family. In the end, Frank the fisherman went to sleep that night, and all you could see on Frank's face through the moonlight coming in from his window was a peaceful smile.

Further Reading

Carveth, D.L. (2010). Superego, Conscience and the Nature and Types of Guilt. Modern Psychoanalysis 35, 1 (2010): 106-130

Freud, A. (1937). The Ego and the mechanisms of defense, London: Hogarth Press and Institute of Psycho-Analysis.

Jacobson E. *Progressive Relaxation,* 2nd Ed. Vol 2. Oxford, England: Univ. Chicago Press; 1938:494.

Acknowledgements

I would like to acknowledge and thank everyone who helped me write this book. First, I would like to thank my family for their love and support that motivates me to pursue this career: my mom, Juana Narvaez, my dad, Felipe Garcia, my sibling, Cesar Garcia, my sibling, Sheyla Hilton, my sibling, Jeshua Garcia, and brother-in-law, Enrique Hilton. They continue to inspire me to become a better version of myself.

A special thanks to my wife, Jessica Garcia, who has been my anchor, my rock, and my main source of support.

Finally, I would like to thank the people who helped me with their time, energy, and intellect to help modify and edit this book: Colette Lau, Vanessa Lau, Kileigh Peturis, and Alexis Wolf, MA, LPC .

About The Author

Jose Garcia-Cuellar, LCSW-S is the owner of Own Your Happiness, a private practice for therapy and coaching. He helps empower people during challenging times in their lives and aids them in healing from trauma.

Jose has been a public speaker for over three years, as well as running a non-profit organization.

The *National Military Empowerment Organization* helps veterans transition into civilian life once they leave service. Jose rose from a childhood of poverty and was the first member of his family to go to college. Once he'd completed grad school, Jose spent months between residences. He filled his days at the public library studying for his license exam, determined to keep moving forward.

Jose is a licensed clinical social worker-supervisor who has helped hundreds of people achieve happiness. Jose's passion is aiding others in overcoming challenges in their lives. When he created a plan for helping his clients eradicate guilt, he knew it was a tool he had to share. He sought a format that would allow others to benefit from and implement his ideas. Jose tried his hand at writing, and it was then the idea for his book *The Guilt Intervention* was born. Though Jose spends most of his time working, he has a passion for learning that plays well in his lifestyle.

Discover more about Jose, his life's work and his books at

www.ownyourhappiness.org

Made in the USA
Columbia, SC
02 December 2024

47143970R00072